MARLEY ABIGAIL

Presents

A Book of Poetry Written From the
Perspective of A Dog by Her Owner

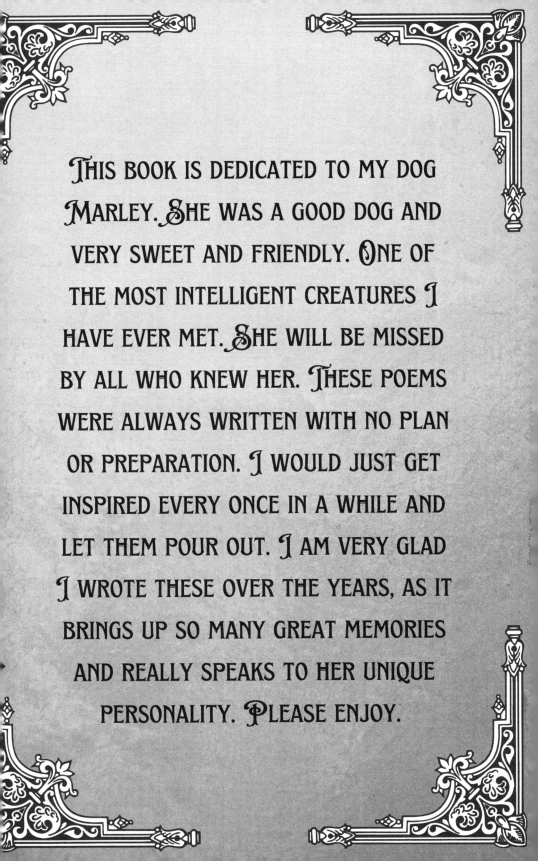

This book is dedicated to my dog Marley. She was a good dog and very sweet and friendly. One of the most intelligent creatures I have ever met. She will be missed by all who knew her. These poems were always written with no plan or preparation. I would just get inspired every once in a while and let them pour out. I am very glad I wrote these over the years, as it brings up so many great memories and really speaks to her unique personality. Please enjoy.

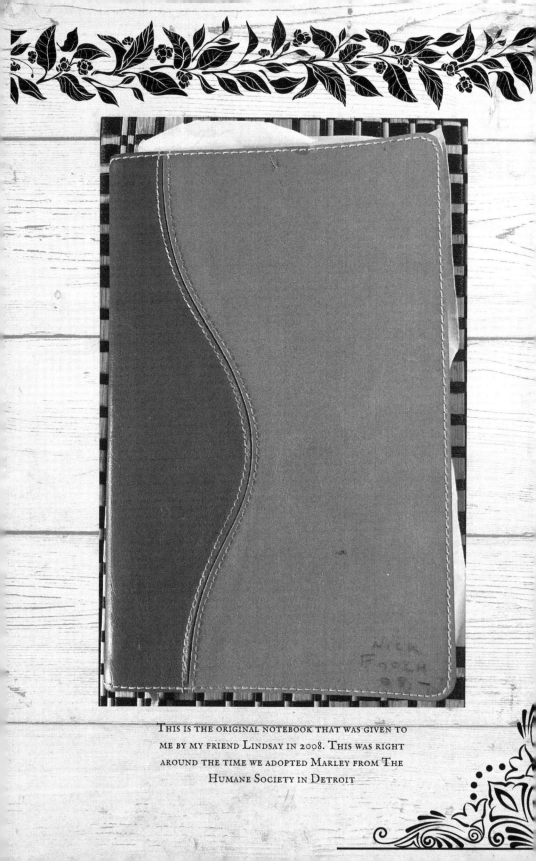

THIS IS THE ORIGINAL NOTEBOOK THAT WAS GIVEN TO ME BY MY FRIEND LINDSAY IN 2008. THIS WAS RIGHT AROUND THE TIME WE ADOPTED MARLEY FROM THE HUMANE SOCIETY IN DETROIT

These poems were written throughout various stages of my dogs life. I hope this book brings as much joy to others as she did.

MARLEY WAS ADOPTED FROM THE
DETROIT HUMANE SOCIETY AT 7
WEEKS OLD. HER NAME THEN WAS
ABIGAIL. WHEN WE MET, SHE
BECAME MARLEY.

🐾🐾🐾🐾🐾🐾🐾🐾🐾🐾🐾

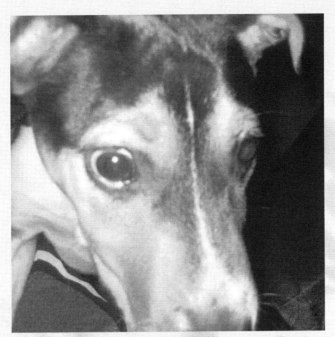

EARLY STAGES

If you are not present during the process of progression, you mind will not process the meaning of the lesson. Some are unaware of the laws they break. This is why soon to be corrected matters appear to be a mistake's. You must follow a path, a code if you will. You must teach right from wrong, with dicipline and skill. Consistency and time will give you a thrill. One step at a time, stay the course, use a leash. If done right it will only take a short while to teach. They grow fast so you must enjoy, one day they will fall, far away from their first toy. It is the life they bring to a broken home, the happiness experienced by observing them chew a bone. On a final note, take care of your pet in the early stages. The reward you will get is worth 1,000 wages.

*marley 5th month inspired poem

12/10/08

Early Stages

If you are not present for the process of progression, your mind will not process the meaning of the lesson.

Some are unaware of the laws that they break. This is why soon to be corrected matters appear to be mistakes.

You must follow a path. A code if you will. You must teach right from wrong, with discipline and skill.

One step ahead. Stay the course. Use a leash. If done right, it will only take a short while to teach.

They grow fast, so you must remember to enjoy. One day they will be far, far away from their first toy.

It is the happiness and life they bring to a broken home. The happiness experienced by simply observing them chew a bone.

On a final note, teach your pet well in the early stages. The rewarded you will get is worth a thousand wages.

December 10, 2008

MARLEY SPEAKS

I got no mother, no sister, no father, no brother. How did we come to find each other? Was I wandering around in the streets alone? Did someone tell you to bring me home? Well, I'm here now and there is nothing I can do. ~~I think~~ I may say though, I'm pleased how I have been treated by you. ~~The~~ I ~~do~~ now have a good house and a place to call home. I am somewhat restricted on where ~~I~~ I may roam, ~~~~ my ~~~~ actions are dictated on words spoke with tone. I am very happy with my home these days, I must wear my lease and not go a stray. Its time to go and has been a great talk, I must no go beg my father for a walk........

1/8/2009

<u>Marley Speaks</u>

I got no mother, no sister, no father, no brother! How did we come to find each other?

Was i wandering around in the streets alone? Did someone tell you to bring me home?

Well, I am here now and there is nothing i can do. I may say though, I am very pleased by how I have been treated by you.

I now have a good house and a place to call home. I am somewhat restricted on where I may roam. My actions are dictated by words spoken with tone.

I am very happy with my life these days. I must wear my leash and not go astray.

It is time for me to go. This has been a great talk. I must now go beg my father for a walk.

January 8, 2009

✿🐾🐾🐾🐾🐾🐾🐾🐾🐾🐾✿

Show? Do you Know?

What once was, is Now Longer.
It HITS with The Force of Someone
Much Stronger. Who will live
Longer amongst The Two. "I am
27 years older Than you!" "Well
I'm a dog, and I age Really
FAST." "But your my Baby and
we are having a Blast."
She Grew Faster Than I Thought,
For her Reputation I STILL FIGHT,
and have Fought. There is Good
I Can See, while other See Bad.
Spend Time, And Be Glad.
Others Dont know The True
Show, you know?

- marley is a good dog
  despite what others may
  say, so ●●●●● all you
  Naysay Sayers.

5/29/19

Show? Do you Know?

What once was is no longer. It hits with the
force of someone much stronger.

Who will live longer amongst the two? I am 27
years older than you!

Well, I am a dog and I age really fast.

But your my dog and we are having a blast.

She grew faster than I thought. For her
reputation I still fight and have fought.

There is good I can see, while others see bad.
Spend as much time as you and be glad.

Others do not know the true show, you know?

Sometime between February 6 – May, 2009

❀ ❀ ❀ ❀ ❀ 🐾 ❀ ❀ ❀ ❀ ❀

Attempted Table Scrap move

There Lived a Dog By The Name of Marley, Her one Dream was To eat Beef Barley. LITTle DID She Know Her Parents DID Not allow. They exclaimed No!" and She Raised "a Brow. "Why Not I may ask" Dog Said With a Gasp." "You Dont GeT Human Food, a Decision made To Let you Live Long at Last" "" ahh I see and I GeT IT, ITs clear. Now may I have a STeak BiT and Perhaps ⬤ ?" "You will Not! as I TolD you Before, NexT Time you ask ITs ~~Us~~ To your Cage With a Closed ~~~~ DOOR "JusT Thought I WoulD Try, you Dont haf To Be RuDe, Speaking of, Can a ⬤ GeT Some More Dog Food.

— 7/10/09

Marley arguing With Master about The Lack Of Human Food in Her LIFe, TesTing The WaTers When She already KnoWs The OuTcome = NO TaBle ScraPs.

Attempted Table Scrap Move

There lives a dog by the name of Marley. Her one
dream was to eat beef barley.

Little did she know, her parents would not allow,
they exclaimed NO! and she raised a brow.

"Why not may I ask?" Marley said with a gasp. "

"You don't get human food. a decision that was made
so you live long and last. "

"Ah, I see. I get it, it's clear. Now may I have a steak
bit and perhaps a pig ear?"

"You will not! I have told you before! Next time you
ask its to your cage with a closed door".

"I just thought I would try, you don't have to be
rude. Speaking of, can this girl get some more dog
food? "

July 10, 2009

*Marley arguing with master about the lack of human
food in her life. Testing the waters when she already
knows the outcome = no table scraps.

🐾🐾🐾🐾🐾🐾🐾🐾🐾🐾

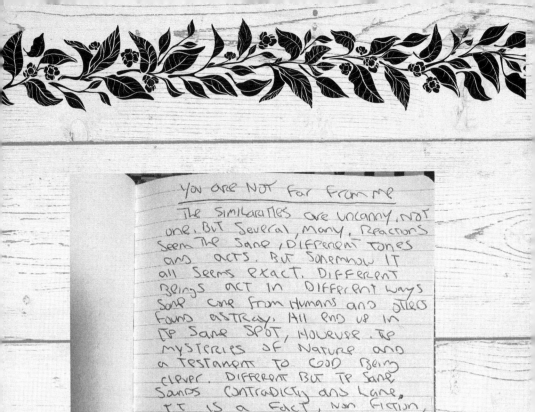

You are NOT Far From me

The similarities are uncanny, Not one, But several, Many, Reactions seem The same, Different tones and acts, But somehow IT all seems exact. Different Beings act in Different ways some one from Humans and others found astray, All end up in Te same Spot, However, Te mysteries of Nature and a Testament to God Being clever, Different But Te same sounds contradicty and Lame. It is a fact, Non Fiction, and is Truely ordained. NO mind your Being or What you are, Fact is your a something That is living, and Friend We are NOT That Far...

— 7/9/09

Humans Shu similar Characteristics To Dags and vice Versa. They are NOT That Far away From each

You Are Not Far From Me

The similarities are uncanny. Not just one but several or many.

Reactions seem the same. Different tones and acts. But somehow it all seems so exact.

Different beings act in different ways. Some come from humans an others found astray.

All will end up in the same spot, however. The mysteries of nature and a testament to god being clever.

Different but the same? Sounds contradicting and lame. It is a fact, non fiction and is truly ordained.

No mind your being or what you are. The fact is you are something that is living and friend, we are not that far apart.

July 9, 2009

*Humans show similar characteristics to dogs and vice versa, they are not that far away from each other.

Older Marley Speaks

I'm older now and I should be free. ~~But~~ Tale off my leash and you will hae to chase me. I eat shoes, rugs, and ████s. Why do you walk me with a pull and a chase.

I ~~will~~ bite without fright of malice intention. My time alone is lonly without mention.

I hae too many toys in a house of clutter. If you want to be lost along provide me with peanut butter. Cage you say!? I dont think so ████ nice try. I dont judge you when youre in Jo business getting ████. Sorry to ████ but its now off my chest. Rub my belly and your nit a crude dad, youre the best!

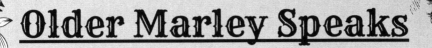

Older Marley Speaks

I am older now and I should be free. Take off my leash and you will have to chase me.

I eat shoes, rugs and sometimes ropes. Why do you walk me with a pull and a choke.

I bite without fright or malice intention. My time alone is lonely without mention.

I have too many toys and a house full of clutter. If you want to be left alone, please provide me with peanut butter.

Into the cage you say?? I don't think so, nice try. I don't judge you when you'r in the basement getting by.

Sorry to complain, but it is now off my chest. Rub my belly and you'r not just a good dad. You'r the best.

Unknown Date, 2009

Marley Speaks......again

Somethg is wrong. What hap

I done today? I think I
_____ up and may go in cage.
It looked good at the time,
the carpet I mean. But I
now know I should not hae
eaten that. now my master
is steamed. He was good
to me and I regret my
actions. I am very glad
He did not hae a bad
reaction. I am alone, restless,
and an outside dog. My
understandng of right and
wrong is an unknown thick fog.
If master gets mad I
know I was bad. I'm
trying to get better so I
can please my dad. I will
now lay down and chew my
bone. should I eat the carpet
while He is on the phone? mybe
He won't see and leae me alone,
I tried but hae faled my
plans are derailed. Guess its true
my bad ways hae sailed.

Marley Speaks..again

Something is wrong. What have I done today? I think I
messed up and may have to go in my cage.

It looked good at the time. The carpet I mean. I know I
should not have eaten that. Now my master is steamed.

He was good to me and I regret my actions. I am very
glad he did not have a bad reaction.

I am alone, restless, and an outside dog. My
understanding of right and wrong is like an unknown
thick fog.

If master gets mad, I know I was bad. I am trying to get
better, so I can please my dad.

I will now lay down and chew my bone. Should I eat the
carpet while he is on the phone? Maybe he wont see and
leave me alone.

I tried but have failed, my plans have been derailed. I
guess it's time my bad ways, like a ship, have sailed.

Unknown Date, 2009

Good Dog

The Beginning Stage is over, No
Time to take the Remainder for
Granted. Best Years are ahead,
in this Regard my view will
not be Slanted. She Brings more
Joy with each Passing Day,
still a Puppy in my eyes on
her Second Birthday. Full of energy,
caring and Calm, Marley wears
her emotions on her Sleeves, Like
a Human with more hardons a Body
littered with 4 arms. Her actions
are Now known, 2881 is
her throne, A Ray of Sunshine
she Becomes when you arrive
home. Good Day or Bad, Happy or
Sad, Tired as ███, and Slow as
a Snail, a Smile on your face
will follow at the sight of miss
abigail. a Bit more predictable
as she continuse to Grow, with
a side of Surprise, a Progresion
we Hope to Be Slow. The slower
the Better, each Day she will Be
embraced, if there was any
Doubt, when you see there, take
a look at your face, when you
Do you will See Joy coupled with
a Smile, we all Hope this will   7/10/2010
last a Long, Long while. - Feliz cumpleaños Abigail
                          Ooh La La

Good Dog

The beginning stage is over. No time to take the remainder for granted. The best years are ahead. In this regard my views will not be slanted.

She brings more joy with each passing day. Still a puppy in my eyes, on her second birthday.

Full of energy, caring, and sometimes calm. Marley wears her emotions on her sleeve. Like a human, but with a lot more hair and less arms.

Her actions are now more known. 28591 Lorraine is where she sits the throne. A ray of sunshine she becomes as you arrive home.

Good day or bad. Happy or sad. Tired as heck and slow as a snail. A smile on your face will follow at the sight of miss Marley Abigail.

A bit more predictable as she continues to grow. A progression to be savored and go very slow.

The slower the better. Each day she will be embraced. If there was any doubt, when you see her, take a look at your face.

When you do, you will see joy coupled with a smile. We all hope it will last a long long while.

July 10, 2010 Marleys 2nd Birthday

I'M NO ROOKIE

Hello Father, Master, Buddy,
whatever. I am more clever
now, older, wiser, and better.
I now know and understand
everything you say. I will play
you like a fiddle, only when
I choose too, I will obey.
All within reason, I will not
be an ████, I just know with
one look I will always get
a pass. I do not take for
granted the life I have.
We all have different routes
to reach our eventuall paths.
Take it easy, big deal, dont
get all high and mighty.
I am a grown dog now, I
still will not bite the. Point
being is that I now have
respect, ████ for the ones who
know me and dont show me
neglect, ████ all the rest.
For they know not what they
see. Hands full of treats one
day, the next day they curse me.
I am grown now, and I
have made my peace. Now where
the ████ is my father with
my ████ ████ leash.

→ Took Marley for a walk immediately after 12:01 AM
— 5/12/11

I'm no Rookie

HELLO FATHER, MASTER, BUDDY, WHATEVER. I AM MORE CLEVER NOW.
OLDER, WISER AND BETTER.

I NOW KNOW AND UNDERSTAND EVERYTHING YOU SAY. I WILL PLAY YOU
LIKE A FIDDLE. ONLY WHEN I CHOOSE TO, I WILL OBEY.

ALL WITHIN REASON. I WILL NOT BE CRASS . I KNOW WITH JUST ONE
LOOK, I WILL ALWAYS GET A PASS.

I DO NOT TAKE FOR GRANTED THE LIFE THAT I HAVE. WE ALL TAKE
DIFFERENT ROUTES TO REACH OUR EVENTUAL PATHS.

TAKE IT EASY, BIG DEAL. DON'T GET ALL HIGH AND MIGHTY. I AM A
GROWN DOG NOW, YOU KNOW ME. I WILL NOT BITE THEE.

THE POINT IS, THAT I NOW HAVE RESPECT. ONLY FOR THOSE WHO
KNOW ME AND DO NOT SHOW ME NEGLECT.

FORGET ALL THE REST. FOR THEY KNOW NOT WHAT THEY SEE.

HAND FULL OF TREATS ONE DAY, AND THE NEXT, THEY CURSE ME.

I AM GROWN NOW AND I HAVE MADE MY PEACE. NOW WHERE IS HECK
IS MY FATHER WITH MY LEASH.

MAY 12, 2011

MARLEY REFLECTS

OLD I am NOT. MANY TRICKS I have LEARNED. I have NOT YET BEGUN. THIS MEETING IS NOT ADJOURNED. I YET REMAIN a PUP, smarter, maybe SET IN MY WAYS. ~~YET~~ YET I have FULL acceptance, approved DAILY BY MY FATHER'S GAZE.

MY Days are SPENT comfortably, absent OF MAJOR FEAT. MY DISH IS always FULL and I LOOK forward TO TREATS. Every Day IS DIFFERENT, NOTHING IS Planned. I am STARTING TO BELIEVE THE HUMANS THINK I UNDERSTAND. THEY SPEAK TO me and I NOD MY HEAD. SOMETIMES I am even allowed TO STEAL THEIR BED. LESS COMPANY THESE DAYS, THIS DOES NOT make me SAD, THE one WHO TAKES CARE OF me IS HOME more OFTEN. THE one I CALL DAD. HE SEEMS TROUBLED THESE DAYS, IN HIS FACE I SEE IT. IT'S Comforting TO KNOW MY PRESENCE always LIFTS HIS SPIRIT. I FEEL BETTER NOW, THIS WAS a NICE TALK, TONIGHT I WILL SLEEP WELL, FX I have already had MY WALK

— 4-5-13

Marley Reflects

Old I am not. Many tricks I have learned. I have not yet begun. This meeting is not adjourned.

I yet remain a pup. Smarter, maybe set in my ways. I now have full acceptance. Approved daily by my fathers gaze.

My days are spent comfortably and absent of any feat. My dish is always full and I look forward to my treats.

Every day is different. Nothing is planned. I am starting to believe that the humans think I understand.

They speak to me and I nod my head. Sometimes I am even allowed to steal their bed.

Less company over these days. This does not make me sad. the one who takes care of me is home more often. The one I call dad.

He seems troubled these days. In his face I can see it. It is comforting to know, that my presence always seems to lift his spirits.

I feel better now. This was a nice talk. I will sleep well tonight. As I have already had my walk.

April 5, 2013

VETERAN DOG LEADERSHIP.

Mellow I have Become BUT I Still have my youth. one Thing Remains, If my chain is Broken, I will Run Loose, I understand The Humans Now, I enjoy when we Talk. My Favorite Part of The Day is still my Daily walk. my food is ~~always~~ always The Same, BUT Now I Think I understand why, Dad wants me Healthy, Doesn't mean I Still won't TRY. while I am alone During The Day I Try To keep Busy, sometimes I Sleep. If I see Strange creatures outsid I Bark, or else I Don't make a Peep.

I have many New TRICKS To LEARN. an old DOG I am NOT. A veteran yes, BUT Still Ready To Be Taught. However, certain Things I already know. BUT I have To Be careful and Still Put on a Show. If I Reveal Too much It will Blow my cover. As long as I appear Teachable They will NOT Seek another. I have HeaRD Good Things are Coming, The Past 3 years were a Bummer. I was Promised By my Dad He is Now able To Drive me To The Park This summer. All in all, I PRETTY much Have ~~no~~ No ~~complaints~~ complaints. Just Happy That we are Both Finally Free of our RESTRAINTS.

3/3/16

Veteran Dog Leadership

Mellow I have become, but I still have my youth. One thing remains. If my chain is broken, I will still run loose.

I understand the humans now. I enjoy it when we talk. My favorite part of the day is still my daily walk.

My food is always the same, but I think I understand why. Dad wants to keep me healthy. It doesn't mean I don't try.

Sometimes I like to just sleep. When I see strange creatures outside, I like to bark, otherwise I won't make a peep.

I have many new tricks to learn. An old dog I am not. A veteran now, yes. Still ready to be taught.

There are many things that I already know. I have to be careful and always put on a show.

If i reveal too much, it will blow my cover. As long as I appear teachable, they will not seek another.

I hear good things are coming. The past three years have been a bummer. I was promised by my dad that he will be able to drive me this summer.

All in all, I have no complaints. I am just happy that me and dad are now both free of our restraints.

March 3, 2016

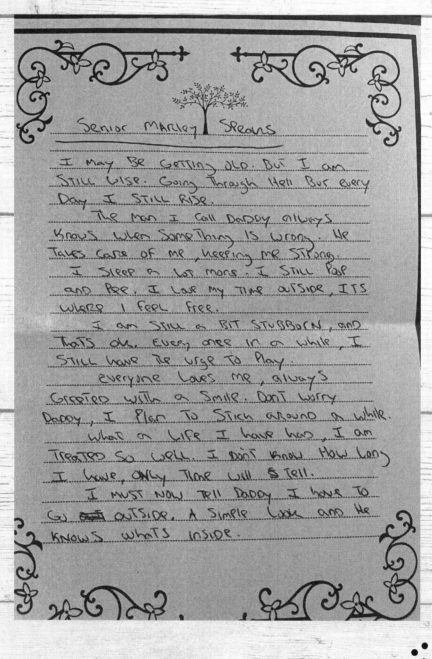

Senior Marley Spears

I may be getting old. But I am still wise. Going through hell but every day I still rise.

The man I call daddy always knows when something is wrong. He takes care of me, keeping me strong.

I sleep a lot more. I still poop and pee, I love my time outside, its where I feel free.

I am still a bit stubborn, and that's ok. Every once in a while, I still have the urge to play.

Everyone loves me, always greeted with a smile. Don't worry daddy, I plan to stick around a while.

What a life I have had, I am treated so well. I don't know how long I have, only time will tell.

I must now tell daddy I have to go outside. A simple look and he knows what's inside.

Senior Marley Speaks

I may be getting older but I am still very wise. Going through hell with cancer but every day I still rise.

The man I call daddy always knows when something is wrong. He takes good care of me. Always keeping me strong.

I sleep a lot more. I still poop and pee. I love my time outside. It is when I feel free.

I am still a bit stubborn and that is ok. Every once in a while, I still have the urge to play.

Everyone loves me. I am always greeted with a smile. Don't worry daddy, I plan to stick around for a while.

What a life I have had. I have been treated so well. I don't know how much longer I have. Only time will tell.

I must now tell my dad that I have to go outside. A simple look and he always knows whats inside.

October, 2021

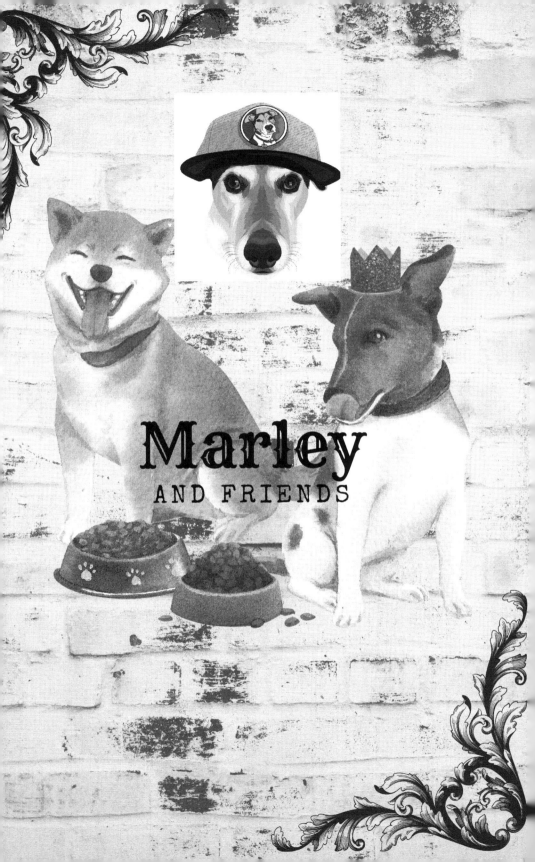

Marley
AND TOYS

FROM A VERY EARLY AGE, MARLEY
ALWAYS LOVED HER TOYS, BONES AND
STUFFED FRIENDS.

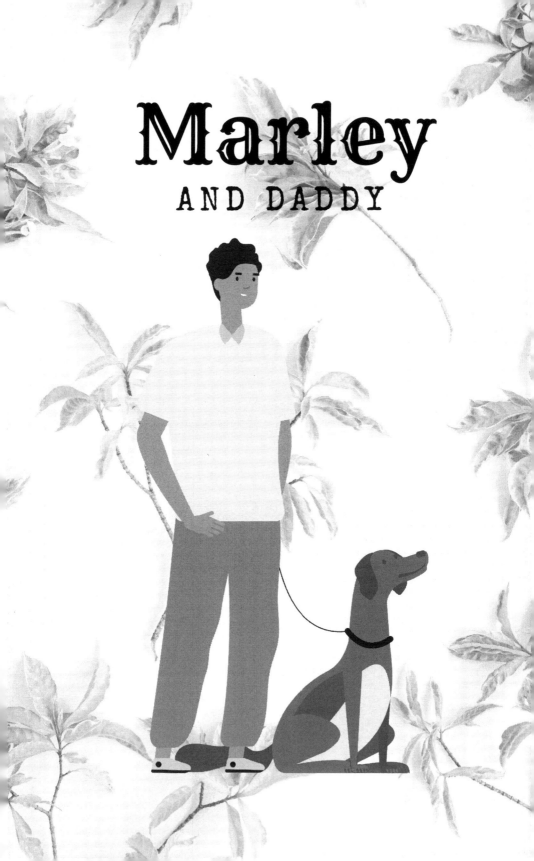

THANK YOU FOR READING!

MARLEYABIGAIL

July 2008 - June 2022

Made in the USA
Columbia, SC
26 January 2023

10313203R00048